Echo Black – A Field Guide to Cyber Espionage

Preface – Read This Before You Begin

This is not a game.

This book is not a manual for criminals. It's a field guide for thinkers for those who understand that knowledge of offensive capability is the cornerstone of meaningful defence... It's a field guide for thinkers for those who understand that knowledge of offensive capability is the cornerstone of meaningful defence.

Echo Black exists to expose the quiet mechanics behind modern espionage operations that shape not only corporate security and geopolitical moves, but also the integrity of systems we depend on every day. These are not theoretical ideas. They are real tactics, modelled from decades of field tradecraft, red team simulations, and threat intelligence analysis. digital operations that shape geopolitics, corporate security, and our everyday lives. These are not theoretical ideas. They are real tactics, modelled from decades of field tradecraft, red team simulations, and threat intelligence analysis.

If you work in security, threat intelligence, or critical infrastructure, this book is your blueprint. If you're a red teamer, pentester, or digital ghost-in-training, this is your edge. And if you're just curious good. Curiosity is where it all begins.

But treat what's inside with respect. Espionage isn't a game. These tools and mindsets carry risk. Use them only where legal, authorised, and ethically sound.

Stay sharp.

Author Notes – A Word from the Shadows

I didn't write this book to be flashy. I wrote it in the quiet hours, where tradecraft lives. After years spent operating in silence, I decided to put the shadows into print... I wrote it because I spent my life learning how the invisible world works, and I believe it's time more people understood it.

Cyber espionage isn't about hacking computers. It's about hacking perception humans, systems, environments, and outcomes. Tools are the medium. Mindset is the weapon... It's about hacking humans, systems, environments, and outcomes. The most effective operators I ever worked with didn't type the fastest or know the most exploits they thought strategically, moved with patience, and understood the value of silence.

This field is evolving. AI is changing the tempo. Attribution is harder. Persistence is quieter. And the lines between attack and defence are almost gone.

But one thing hasn't changed: discipline. This book is dedicated to those who approach the craft with honour, restraint, and clarity of purpose.

Be ruthless in your study. Be selective in your application. Be invisible in your execution.

– Silas Vire

Table of Contents

Foreword

In the shadowy crossroads of cyberspace and covert operations lies a new theatre of warfare one not fought with bullets or boots, but with keystrokes, crafted exploits, and an intimate understanding of human behaviour. This isn't theory. This isn't Hollywood. This is reality.

Echo Black is a boots-on-digital-ground field guide, forged in the fire of operational pressure and shaped by lived experience. It's grounded in brutal discipline designed not to dazzle, but to prepare.

Cyber espionage has become a dominant battlefield for nations, corporations, and criminal syndicates alike. Whether you're an up-and-coming red team operator, a seasoned intelligence analyst, or a cybersecurity professional ready to go beyond textbook jargon, this book walks you through real tradecraft the techniques, the mindset, and the discipline required to move undetected through adversarial territory.

During my years in the field, silence was my weapon, invisibility my shield, and information my prize. What follows is a distillation of that world. It is not written to entertain. It is written to prepare.

You won't find flashy exploits for their own sake here. Everything discussed has been selected for its effectiveness, tested in live environments, and deployed under pressure. This is about capability not spectacle.

The mission of *Echo Black* is simple: to arm the next generation of cyber operatives with the knowledge, mindset, and operational finesse to thrive in the invisible war. We leave theory behind. We discard the buzzwords. And we get to work.

If you're ready to operate in the shadows welcome aboard.

Welcome to the shadows.

Chapter 1: Tradecraft Reborn – The Evolution of Espionage

Long before firewalls and intrusion detection systems, espionage relied on lockpicks, false identities, and encoded microdots. In the trenches of the Cold War, and long before that, spies operated with physical tools, psychological manipulation, and unflinching discipline. Their missions were slow, methodical, and dangerous yet the principles behind them endure. Today, in the age of cyber warfare, tradecraft has shifted from alleys to IP addresses, but the foundations remain: access, stealth, and control.

This chapter marks the true beginning of our journey. We'll explore how classical tradecraft has morphed into digital operations and why understanding this evolution is critical to mastering cyber espionage. It's not about the tools it's about the method. It's about mindset.

From Brush Passes to Packet Sniffers

A brush pass in a crowded city square has evolved into an encrypted file drop on a compromised server. Where surveillance once meant hours hidden in a parked car with a telephoto lens, it now means activating a hijacked webcam from half a world away. The dead drop has become a malware payload. Different methods same mission: deliver or extract sensitive material without exposing the source.

Classical Roots, Digital Execution

Many of today's most capable cyber operatives began with or were trained in the traditions of classical espionage. They understand that deception, social engineering, and patience remain at the heart of every successful intrusion. A convincingly spoofed email can open more doors than the most advanced zero-day exploit. A synthetic online persona, complete with a backstory and digital footprint, is the modern forged passport. Tradecraft remains psychological as much as it is technical.

Tradecraft Principles in the Digital Domain

- **Access**: Penetrating a network, device, or human interface be it through a phishing lure, credential stuffing, or social engineering. Every operation begins with that first foothold.

- **Stealth**: Operating undetected, using encrypted channels, anti-forensic techniques, living-off-the-land binaries, and blending into normal system behaviour. The best operations are invisible.

- **Control**: Sustaining presence, pivoting across systems, escalating access, and guiding the operation from intrusion to exfiltration all while remaining in the shadows.

These pillars aren't optional they are the mission blueprint. Advanced technology changes the tactics, but never the tradecraft.

Why It Matters

Tradecraft is not just historical it's instructional. Every evolution in espionage was born out of failure, correction, and necessity. As you move through this field guide, you'll see how age-old spy techniques live on in code, proxies, and decoys. Cyber espionage isn't a computer science it's an operational art.

We are not discarding our roots we're adapting them. The same mission persists: know your target, blend into the noise, and extract value without ever being seen.

This is the new theatre of espionage.

Chapter 2: Cyber Espionage Operations – Anatomy of a Digital Intrusion

In cyber espionage, nothing is left to chance. Behind every breach, every stolen credential, and every vanished file lies a deliberate, methodical campaign a digital intrusion mapped and executed with surgical precision. This chapter dissects that operation phase by phase, providing a blueprint that every operator offensive or defensive must master.

Understanding the lifecycle of an intrusion is not just about knowing how attackers think; it's about anticipating their every move. This is your operational map one that shows how to plan, execute, or disrupt digital espionage from end to end.

Phase 1: Reconnaissance – Know Your Target

Every mission starts with intelligence gathering. Open-source intelligence (OSINT), social media profiles, domain registries, credential leaks, and job postings all help paint a comprehensive picture. Passive reconnaissance avoids detection; active techniques, like port scanning and banner grabbing, yield technical insights. The goal is simple: profile the target completely before engaging.

Phase 2: Initial Access – Breaching the Perimeter

With knowledge in hand, the next step is to break in. Common intrusion methods include:

- Spear phishing emails embedded with payloads

- Exploiting unpatched vulnerabilities (CVEs)

- Credential stuffing using known password leaks

- Social engineering (phone pretexting, impersonated IT support)

This is a high-risk stage. A misstep here could compromise the entire operation. Precision and subtlety are paramount.

Phase 3: Establishing Foothold – Persistence Begins

With the perimeter breached, the operation now transitions from entry to establishment. This is where the groundwork laid in the previous phase must be solidified into sustained access. The shift is seamless one moment of success must immediately be leveraged to create lasting presence. Once inside, continued access is critical. This stage ensures the operator isn't evicted by a reboot or security sweep. Techniques include:

- Deploying Remote Access Trojans (RATs)

- Creating hidden scheduled tasks or cron jobs

- Abusing legitimate admin tools (LotL techniques)

A foothold becomes the operator's safe house. It marks the shift from penetration to occupation.

Phase 4: Privilege Escalation & Internal Recon

Initial access is rarely enough. The operator must elevate privileges to reach sensitive data. Methods include:

- Exploiting local misconfigurations or privilege escalation bugs

- Harvesting stored credentials and tokens

- Pass-the-hash, token impersonation, and abusing SUID/Sticky Bits

With elevated rights, internal recon begins: mapping network topology, discovering trust relationships, and identifying valuable systems.

Phase 5: Lateral Movement – Expanding the Operation

The operator now pivots through the environment. Movement may involve:

- Using RDP, SMB, WMI, or SSH to access other hosts

- Leveraging domain trusts and misconfigured permissions

- Targeting backup controllers, domain admins, or isolated enclaves

Each hop deepens access but increases exposure. Lateral movement is both opportunity and danger.

Phase 6: Data Collection & Exfiltration

With access and targets aligned, the core mission begins exfiltrating valuable data:

- Blueprints, credentials, emails, financials, IP, or full VM images

Common exfiltration strategies include:

- Covert C2 channels (DNS tunnelling, HTTPS beaconing)

- Fragmenting and staging data across systems

- Obfuscating payloads within legitimate-looking traffic (e.g., steganography or protocol misuse)

Phase 7: Covering Tracks – Erase the Footprint

A skilled operator leaves no trace. Counter-forensics includes:

- Clearing logs and shell history

- Timestomping, log poisoning, and hiding binaries

- Scrubbing telemetry and forensic artefacts

Cleaning up isn't an afterthought it's the difference between success and exposure.

Every successful digital intrusion follows a strict, layered sequence. Each phase builds upon the last, much like a surgeon advancing step by step through a carefully orchestrated procedure with discipline and intent. Just as a surgeon follows a procedure, a cyber operative adheres to a plan.

Learn the rhythm. Respect the phases. Because in cyber espionage, your mastery of this anatomy determines whether you remain in the shadows or become someone's case study.

Chapter 3: Targeting & Reconnaissance

Reconnaissance lays the foundation of every cyber espionage operation long before a single packet is fired or a phishing email sent, reconnaissance lays the foundation of every cyber espionage operation. It is the art of knowing your target without alerting them to your presence. Precision targeting starts with intelligence, not tools. In the old world, it meant watching routines, following subjects, and intercepting communications. In the digital domain, it means quietly harvesting information from open sources, breached data, and the target's own exposure.

A successful recon phase sets the tone for the entire operation. The more complete the picture, the lower the risk and the higher the success rate. This chapter breaks down how to identify, profile, and map your target before you even consider moving in.

The Objective: Building the Target Dossier

Targeting begins with intent. What are you after financials, credentials, insider access, proprietary intelligence? Understanding the value determines how deep you need to go. Once this is clear, the next step is assembling your dossier. This includes:

- Corporate structure and business units
- Technology stack (servers, endpoints, cloud services)
- Key personnel, roles, and reporting lines
- Physical locations and network topology
- Past breaches or security incidents

This intelligence isn't gathered through guesswork or brute-force tactics. It's derived from deliberate, low-noise methods that avoid tipping off the target. It's harvested with surgical care.

OSINT: The Passive Hunter's Toolkit

Open Source Intelligence (OSINT) is your starting ground. From job ads and press releases to DNS records and social media profiles, OSINT exposes the soft underbelly of even hardened targets.

- WHOIS and domain history
- Employee LinkedIn profiles
- Shodan and Censys device fingerprints
- Pastebin, GitHub, and code leaks

- Email breach databases and credential dumps

The art lies in correlation connecting dots others overlook.

With your OSINT framework established, the next layer of intelligence gathering comes through passive reconnaissance stealth observation without touching the target directly.

Passive Reconnaissance

In cyber espionage, stealth is everything. Passive recon avoids direct interaction with the target's systems. The aim is to gather technical and human intelligence without triggering alarms:

- DNS harvesting and subdomain enumeration

- SSL certificate transparency logs

- Dark web monitoring for related chatter

- Monitoring social engineering exposure points

Every piece of data paints the target sharper, but the brushstroke must be invisible.

Active Reconnaissance

Once you've exhausted passive means, light-touch active techniques can refine the profile:

- Banner grabbing

- Port scanning with noise throttling (e.g., Masscan, Nmap)

- HTTP/S header analysis

- Response behaviour profiling (e.g., error codes, load balancing hints)

Here, timing, frequency, and tool configuration matter. The line between insight and detection is razor-thin.

Human-Centric Targeting

People are often the path of least resistance. Understanding human targets through social media, online habits, and organisational structure can yield:

- Likely credentials based on patterns

- Ideal phishing pretexts

- Key influencers and decision-makers

- Misconfigured personal devices linked to corporate networks

This isn't just profiling. It's the quiet hunt for human weak points in a digital chain.

Toolsets for Recon

Before diving into tools, remember this: they are force multipliers, not replacements for sound thinking. While mindset drives recon, tools amplify its scale and precision. Operators should be proficient with:

- **theHarvester** for email, domain, and subdomain collection

- **Maltego** for link analysis and relationship mapping

- **SpiderFoot** for automated OSINT

- **Amass** for domain enumeration

- **Recon-ng** for structured recon workflows

The tool is not the operator. It's the brush, not the artist.

Closing the Loop: Target Validation

Before moving on, the dossier must be verified. Targets are validated not just by availability, but by vulnerability and value alignment. Ask:

- Can this be accessed without detection?

- Will this provide the desired intelligence?

- Are the risks of engagement acceptable?

A poorly validated target leads to wasted effort or worse, exposure. Precision at this stage safeguards the entire operation.

Reconnaissance is more than preparation it is the prelude to every victory. In the world of espionage, the operation begins long before the breach. The shadows favour those who watch carefully.

Next comes the breach itself an act that rewards only those with the patience and discipline to plan with precision. But those who rush to fire before they aim never last long in this game.

Chapter 4: Initial Access – Breaching the Perimeter

Every operation builds toward a single critical juncture: the breach. After the deliberate, methodical work of reconnaissance, the operative transitions from silent observer to active infiltrator. This is where skill meets nerve where planning turns into execution. the breach. After the patient build-up of intelligence and reconnaissance, the operator moves from observer to actor. This phase, initial access, is where skill meets nerve. A misstep here risks burning the operation before it even begins. But a well-executed breach opens the gates to everything that follows.

Initial access isn't about brute force or theatrical exploits it's about strategy. Exploiting trust, targeting weak links, and slipping in without setting off alarms is the mark of a seasoned operator. it's about exploiting trust, leveraging overlooked weaknesses, and slipping through the cracks unnoticed. This chapter unpacks the real-world methods used to breach digital perimeters, emphasising stealth, timing, and deception over noise.

The Art of Entry

No two environments are the same, and the method of entry depends on the intelligence gathered during reconnaissance. A phishing email may be enough for one target. For another, it may require a multi-step supply chain attack. The goal is the same: gain a foothold without tripping any wires.

Common initial access vectors include:

- **Spear Phishing**: Tailored emails with malicious links or attachments exploiting human trust.

- **Credential Reuse**: Using leaked passwords from other breaches to authenticate into systems.

- **Exploiting Public-Facing Vulnerabilities**: Targeting unpatched web applications, VPNs, or cloud interfaces.

- **Drive-by Compromise**: Planting malicious code in websites likely to be visited by the target.

- **Social Engineering**: Pretexting phone calls, impersonating vendors or IT personnel.

- **Supply Chain Compromise**: Inserting malicious components or updates into trusted third-party software.

Timing and Context

Drawing directly from the insights gathered in reconnaissance, timing becomes a weapon in itself. The difference between a detected attack and a silent intrusion often lies in when and how the operator acts. Attacks launched during public holidays, system updates, or shift changes tend to fly under the radar. The more embedded your intelligence is in the target's behaviour and routines, the more surgical your strike can be.

Patience here is not weakness. It's strategy.

Weaponisation and Delivery

Initial access typically requires the use of a payload malicious software designed to give control or access once delivered. But even the payload must be disguised:

- **Macro-enabled Documents**: Malicious Office files disguised as internal memos or invoices.

- **Malicious PDFs**: Weaponised documents crafted to exploit reader vulnerabilities.

- **Executable Wrappers**: Embedding payloads in seemingly benign applications or installers.

- **HTA and JS Files**: Scripting techniques used to trigger execution on user interaction.

Each delivery method must be tailored to the target's habits, systems, and defences. One-size-fits-all doesn't exist here.

Avoiding Detection

Breaching the perimeter is only half the job. Remaining unseen once inside is what defines a successful operation. The most dangerous threat is the one you never see. Operators use every trick to blend in:

- Domain fronting and spoofed email headers

- Payload encryption and obfuscation

- Living-off-the-land binaries for stealthy execution

- DNS tunnelling or HTTPS for covert command and control

Initial access must feel like nothing at all just another click, another email, another day in the network.

Foot in the Door

Achieving initial access is like slipping a lock quiet, precise, and intentional. It's not the endgame. It's the start of one. From this point on, persistence and escalation become the focus. But none of that matters if you don't make it through the door.

The breach is the threshold between theory and action where everything learned, planned, and prepared must converge. It's the moment that separates the opportunist from the professional. Execute it wrong, and you vanish in a puff of alerts. Execute it right, and you're inside with no one the wiser... All your recon, all your targeting, builds to this moment. Execute it wrong, and you vanish in a puff of alerts. Execute it right, and you're inside with no one the wiser.

Next, we turn to what happens after you're in: establishing persistence, maintaining control, and laying the groundwork for deeper operations.

Chapter 5: Persistence & Control – Holding the Beachhead

Initial access marks the turning point from breacher to occupier. Once the perimeter is breached, the mission becomes one of quiet longevity. It's about embedding deeply, sustaining presence, and ensuring that access isn't just gained it's held with precision and purpose... Once the perimeter is breached, the mission shifts to maintaining access quietly and reliably. This is the phase were operators transition from opportunists to occupiers. It's about establishing presence, embedding deeply, and ensuring that access isn't just temporary, but resilient.

Persistence isn't about remaining present it's about becoming invisible while staying in control. In the world of cyber espionage, the best presence is the one they never know is there. it's about staying undetected while maintaining a silent foothold. This chapter breaks down the tactics used to ensure long-term access, maintain command and control, and manipulate the compromised environment to your advantage.

The Objective: Stay In, Stay Hidden

Persistence is a balancing act: remain undetected while ensuring you can return at will. It means preparing fallback methods, building redundant access points, and mimicking legitimate behaviour so closely that even trained analysts overlook you.

This is where stealth escalates to craft.

Persistence Mechanisms

Operators employ various techniques to establish footholds that survive reboots, user logins, and system updates:

- **Scheduled Tasks / Cron Jobs**: Periodic execution of malware disguised as system tasks.

- **Registry Run Keys & Startup Items**: Auto-launch mechanisms on Windows and Linux.

- **Service Hijacking**: Replacing or injecting malicious code into legitimate services.

- **Browser Extensions / Add-ons**: Used for credential theft and backdoor execution.

- **Hidden User Accounts**: Accounts created and concealed from casual administrative review.

- **Firmware Implants**: Rare but powerful, these survive OS reinstalls and low-level wipes.

Command and Control (C2)

If persistence is the foundation, command and control is the lifeline. It's what allows an operator to maintain influence over the environment, issue new orders, and adapt to changing conditions all without breaking cover. Maintaining communication with the compromised host is essential for issuing commands, retrieving data, or triggering secondary payloads. Stealthy C2 techniques include:

- **HTTPS Tunnelling**: Blends in with normal web traffic.

- **DNS Tunnelling**: Covert data transfer using domain name queries.

- **Social Media Channels**: Commands embedded in Twitter posts, GitHub gists, or YouTube comments.

- **Custom Protocols over Standard Ports**: Masquerading as legitimate applications.

C2 must be adaptive capable of fallback, encryption, and blending into regular traffic profiles.

Living Off the Land (LotL)

This is the art of making the environment your toolkit. LotL techniques are not only stealthy they're effective because defenders often overlook what they consider 'normal' system activity. Instead of bringing their own tools, advanced operators use what's already available in the target environment:

- **PowerShell, WMIC, CertUtil**: Powerful scripting and file transfer utilities.

- **Scheduled jobs, bash scripts, service configs**: Local persistence and recon aids.

- **Remote Management Frameworks**: Leveraging legitimate admin tools to avoid detection.

LotL techniques are harder to detect and investigate, especially when commands appear indistinguishable from legitimate admin activity.

Evading Detection & Anti-Forensics

The longer you stay, the greater the risk. Persistence without detection requires:

- **Timestomping and Log Manipulation**: Altering or erasing audit trails.

- **Fileless Malware Techniques**: Keeping code in memory, avoiding disk writes.

- **User Behaviour Mimicry**: Operating only during known user activity hours.

- **Randomised Check-ins**: Avoiding regular network beacons that create patterns.

Anti-forensics isn't paranoia it's operational hygiene.

Redundancy & Recovery

No access point is bulletproof. Skilled operators prepare for loss of foothold:

- **Multiple Persistence Vectors**: If one is discovered, others remain.

- **Decentralised C2 Nodes**: Eliminating single points of failure.

- **Self-Healing Payloads**: Scripts or implants that reinstate access if removed.

Persistence is not a single technique it's an ecosystem of survival.

Establishing access is one thing. Holding it undetected is another. In espionage, presence is power but only if no one knows you're there. The ability to persist, command, and adapt without exposure defines the strength of your operation.

Next, we go deeper. Escalation and expansion are the natural evolution of persistence. The beachhead is secure now it's time to move through the network like smoke through cracks in stone... Privilege escalation and lateral movement await. The beachhead is held now it's time to expand the territory.

Chapter 6: Privilege Escalation & Lateral Movement – Expanding the Operation

Establishing persistence is only the first milestone like breaching the wall of a fortress. But real control comes from what happens next: expansion. Once inside, the operator must move both vertically and laterally, climbing the chain of command and spreading quietly through the digital terrain... Once inside, an operator must move beyond the initial foothold vertically and laterally. Privilege escalation is about gaining more control within a compromised system. Lateral movement is about spreading that control across the network. Together, they enable deep penetration, long-term access, and operational flexibility.

This is where access becomes power.

Privilege Escalation – Climbing the Ladder

With the beachhead secured, the next phase begins: expanding your influence. Privilege escalation provides the leverage needed to elevate access and unlock deeper operational capability. Operators often start with limited user access. Elevating those privileges unlocks administrative control, allowing for deeper reconnaissance, tool deployment, and full control over system behaviours.

Common escalation techniques include:

- **Exploiting Local Vulnerabilities**: Kernel exploits, misconfigured SUID binaries, or driver-level flaws.

- **Credential Dumping**: Extracting hashes, tokens, or cleartext passwords from memory or registry.

- **Pass-the-Hash / Pass-the-Ticket**: Using captured credentials to impersonate users without cracking them.

- **Token Impersonation**: Assuming the identity of privileged processes.

- **Scheduled Task Abuse / DLL Hijacking**: Leveraging misconfigured services or execution paths.

Escalation should be quiet no sudden system crashes, no unexpected reboots. Silence is success.

Mapping the Internal Landscape

You can't dominate what you don't understand. Elevated access opens the door to network intelligence—allowing you to navigate, analyse, and exploit the digital terrain with surgical precision. With elevated access comes the ability to map the internal network in greater detail:

- Enumerate internal subnets, DNS zones, and trust relationships

- Identify high-value systems: domain controllers, databases, jump boxes

- Review system configurations, installed software, and patch levels

- Analyse user and group memberships for lateral pivot opportunities

Network discovery should follow the least noise principle: targeted scans, native tools, and timing that mimics legitimate admin activity.

Lateral Movement – Spreading the Reach

Privilege escalation is vertical. Lateral movement is horizontal. The goal is to reach systems of strategic value, hop-by-hop, without raising alarms.

Techniques include:

- **Remote Desktop Protocol (RDP)**: Common for manual interaction but highly monitored.

- **Windows Management Instrumentation (WMI)** and **PsExec**: Powerful remote execution via Windows features.

- **SMB / File Shares**: Transferring payloads or pivoting through misconfigured shares.

- **SSH / Remote Shells**: Leveraging known credentials or key-based access.

- **Exploiting Trust Relationships**: Crossing domains or business units using existing permissions.

Each move should blend into the background. Stealth over speed remains the guiding principle every pivot should mimic legitimate activity so well that even active defenders dismiss it as noise., using native protocols and tools whenever possible.

Persistence Across Systems

As the operator moves laterally, new footholds should be quietly established:

- Deploy lightweight persistence on each system

- Stagger command and control traffic to avoid patterns

- Rotate or diversify C2 infrastructure to prevent correlation

Movement without foothold is temporary. Each step must secure a new anchor point.

Operational Security at Scale

Expanding access multiplies exposure. To remain undetected:

- Avoid simultaneous logins across systems

- Mimic legitimate traffic patterns and login hours

- Disable or clean up forensic artefacts after pivoting

- Monitor and adjust based on defender activity or alerts

Good operators don't just think about the next system they think about how every action echoes through the network.

Privilege escalation and lateral movement are the engine room of long-term espionage. They convert access into influence, and influence into dominance. Without control over the broader environment, persistence is just squatting. Real power is the ability to move, adapt, and command.

Next, we shift to the true objective of most campaigns: data. The mission now enters its most delicate stage collection and exfiltration. The operator becomes the ghost, moving through the environment unseen, gathering intelligence, and preparing to vanish without a trace.: the data itself. It's time to collect, extract, and vanish without a trace.

Chapter 7: Data Exfiltration & Covering Tracks – Vanishing Without a Trace

Everything in the operation has led to this final, critical juncture. Months of preparation, stealth, and surgical execution have brought the operator to the edge of their objective. Success now hinges on the most fragile phase extracting the data without setting off a single alarm... The breach was silent. Persistence was secured. Privileges were elevated, and movement through the environment was surgical. Now, it's time to achieve the objective: extract valuable intelligence and leave no trace behind.

Exfiltration is the culmination of the mission. It's where planning meets execution. But success here isn't just about getting the data it's about getting it out cleanly, quietly, and without triggering the tripwires that defenders leave waiting.

Identifying the Crown Jewels

Before exfiltration, an operator must determine what matters most. That means:

- Intellectual property (designs, formulas, source code)

- Credential stores and authentication tokens

- Emails, documents, and communications archives

- Database dumps and customer data

- Financial records or strategic plans

Prioritising target data reduces risk. More noise means more eyes.

Staging the Payload

Before data can be moved, it must be handled with care. Staging ensures that exfiltration appears as normal network behaviour not a smash-and-grab operation. Data rarely leaves a network all at once. It's collected, compressed, and staged often across several systems to prepare for extraction:

- **Data Chunking**: Breaking large files into smaller encrypted pieces.

- **Compression & Encryption**: Zip or 7z files with strong passwords and hidden file names.

- **Staging Hosts**: Using compromised systems as intermediaries to hold or forward data.

Good staging ensures minimal bandwidth spikes, few anomalies, and plausible system behaviour.

Exfiltration Techniques

No single technique works in every environment. The method chosen must reflect what the operator knows about the network's defences, detection thresholds, and behavioural baselines. Stealth is paramount. The method of extraction depends on the environment and its monitoring controls:

- **HTTPS Exfiltration**: Encrypted web traffic hides data in plain sight.

- **DNS Tunnelling**: Covert channels via domain queries.

- **Cloud Sync Abuse**: Leveraging legitimate sync clients (e.g. Dropbox, Google Drive).

- **Social Media Channels**: Posting encoded data in comments or commits.

- **Steganography**: Embedding files within images, videos, or documents.

- **Email Exfiltration**: Auto-drafted messages saved to synced outboxes.

Success means the data moves as quietly as the operator did.

Anti-Forensics – Cleaning Up

Once the data is gone, the focus shifts to erasing every footprint. Anti-forensics is the surgical cleanup the quiet dismantling of the operator's presence. With the payload gone, the operation enters its most delicate stage erasure. Anti-forensic measures aim to erase footprints and kill attribution:

- **Log Clearing & Timestomping**: Deleting or altering timestamps and event logs.

- **Script Self-Destruction**: Payloads and droppers that erase themselves post-execution.

- **Clearing Shell Histories**: Cleaning up bash, PowerShell, or remote access session trails.

- **Removing Persistence**: Once data is secured, any remaining implants are pulled or destroyed.

The goal is to vanish like smoke. Not a backdoor. Not a beacon. Nothing.

Timing the Exit

Exfiltration is not always the end. Some operators stay for ongoing access. Others disappear immediately. The key is knowing when to go:

- **After Scheduled Downtimes**: Maintenance windows hide anomalies.

- **At Night / Off-Hours**: Reduces chance of immediate detection.

- **Following Decoy Events**: Other network noise can be used to mask the exit.

A good exit is one the defenders never realise happened until it's far too late.

This is the apex of the operation where every decision must be flawless. Anyone can infiltrate. Only the elite vanish like they were never there... The point where skill, patience, and precision collide. Anyone can break in. The elite know how to get out clean.

Next, we dive into the art of counterintelligence detecting spies, deceiving attackers, and turning the tables inside the networks they think they own.

Chapter 8: Countering the Spy – Defensive Cyber Tradecraft

Offence may dominate headlines, but true control is forged in defence. This is where resilience is architected not through firewalls alone, but through mindset. Counter-espionage isn't reactive. It's anticipatory. In this chapter, we flip the script. You're no longer the infiltrator you're the hunter. Your task is to expose, deceive, and dismantle threats that have already slipped past the gates... Counter-espionage is not just about detecting intrusions it's about thinking like a spy to catch one. In this chapter, we flip the script. You're no longer the operator you're the hunter. Your job is to expose, isolate, and eliminate threats hiding inside your network.

Defensive tradecraft is about discipline, visibility, and deception. You're not just responding to incidents you're anticipating them, detecting anomalies before they become breaches, and designing your systems to resist, reveal, and recover.

Threat Hunting vs Passive Defence

To think like a hunter, you must anticipate the tactics of a spy. The goal is not to catch malware it's to catch intent. Traditional security often relies on alerts and logs to flag known threats. But today's adversaries aren't firing off loud malware they're hiding in memory, living off the land, and mimicking administrators.

Threat hunting flips the model. It's proactive, continuous, and intelligence-driven. You don't wait for signs of compromise you investigate without a known IOC (Indicator of Compromise):

- Monitor abnormal lateral movement patterns

- Track unusual command usage (e.g., WMIC, CertUtil, PowerShell)

- Flag inconsistent login behaviour across time zones or work hours

- Audit trusted accounts for misuse or overuse

The best defenders don't wait. They hunt.

Telemetry and Visibility

You can't stop what you can't see. Visibility is foundational. Defensive teams must collect rich telemetry from:

- Endpoint Detection and Response (EDR) platforms

- System logs (auth, kernel, application)

- Network traffic (flow, packet, DNS, SSL inspection)

- Cloud APIs and audit trails

Correlating these signals reveals the patterns that spies can't entirely hide.

Behavioural Detection over Signature-Based

Signature-based detection is only as strong as its database. But elite actors rewrite the rules, repack the tools, and slip past known patterns. Modern adversaries mutate constantly. Hashes change. Payloads shift. Signatures break.

Behaviour, however, betrays them. Behavioural detection focuses on *what* an actor does, not *how* they're encoded:

- Persistence creation in uncommon registry paths

- Scripts executing through Office macros

- Command-line usage that chains reconnaissance and exfiltration

- Sudden access to multiple critical systems from a single host

Even advanced attackers leave behavioural fingerprints.

Setting Traps – Defensive Deception

Deception is the art of turning offence into defence. By weaponizing curiosity and expectation, you give attackers exactly what they want on your terms. Sometimes, the best way to catch an intruder is to lure them in.

Deception technologies turn the network against the attacker:

- **Honeypots**: Decoy systems designed to attract and log malicious behaviour.

- **Honeytokens**: Fake credentials or files planted in legitimate environments.

- **Canary Accounts / Documents**: Alerts triggered when a decoy is accessed.

- **DNS Sinkholes**: Fake domains to intercept outbound C2 traffic.

When done well, these tools don't just detect they disorient.

Response with Precision

Detection without response is just knowledge. Once a spy is found, the response must be:

- **Surgical**: Avoid tipping off the attacker too early.

- **Coordinated**: Legal, HR, IT, and security must align.

- **Measured**: Consider isolating, monitoring longer for intelligence gains.

- **Final**: When it's time to strike contain, clean, and eradicate.

The mission isn't just to stop them it's to understand them. Their tools, their methods, their objectives.

To beat a spy, you must become a better one. Defensive cyber tradecraft isn't just about survival it's about disruption. The more you think like an attacker, the more you reshape the battlefield in your favour. Defence becomes offence, and every misstep the enemy makes becomes your opportunity... Defensive cyber tradecraft is not just a shield it's a mirror, reflecting the enemy's playbook back at them. The more you think like an attacker, the harder it becomes for one to live inside your network.

Next, we explore the power of deception not just to detect, but to manipulate, mislead, and control the adversary's narrative.

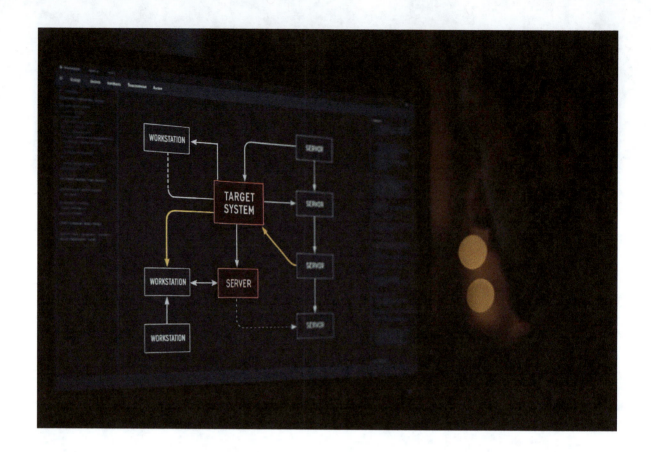

Chapter 9: Deception & Misdirection – Turning the Network Against Them

Deception isn't just a tactic it's the reclamation of initiative. It shifts the balance of power from intruder to defender by creating uncertainty, false confidence, and carefully crafted traps that exploit the attacker's own instincts... It shifts the balance of power from the intruder to the defender by introducing uncertainty, false confidence, and traps that exploit the attacker's assumptions. In this chapter, we weaponize misdirection.

The goal isn't just to detect. It's to control. Deception allows defenders to influence attacker behaviour, shape decisions, and gather intelligence—all without the adversary realising they're being manipulated.

The Philosophy of Misdirection

At its core, deception is about control. You control the information, the environment, and the timing. You decide what looks real, what looks vulnerable, and what leads to dead ends.

Every good operator knows how to mislead a target. Defensive misdirection uses that same principle in reverse:

- Create doubt about what's real and what's bait

- Lead attackers into false confidence

- Frustrate and fatigue with dead ends and junk data

If they waste time, reveal tools, or trigger alerts you're winning.

Deceptive Infrastructure

Realism is everything. The more authentic your decoys, the more time an attacker spends interacting with them giving defenders visibility, context, and time to respond. Creating realistic decoys is more than spinning up a spare VM. Effective deception requires depth, consistency, and plausibility:

- **Honeynets**: Full subnet simulations with realistic traffic and vulnerabilities

- **Fake Databases**: Populated with credible (but fake) financial, personnel, or credential data

- **Decoy Credentials**: Injected into memory, config files, or browser storage

- **DNS and Email Traps**: Domains and addresses monitored for unexpected use

The more believable the trap, the more valuable the intelligence it collects.

Instrumenting the Attacker

This is where deception moves from passive defence to active intelligence gathering. The attacker becomes the source, and every click tells a story. Deception is also about surveillance. Every interaction with a decoy is a lesson:

- **Tool Fingerprinting**: Log what scanners, malware, or exploits are used

- **TTP Discovery**: Learn the adversary's techniques, tactics, and procedures

- **Intent Mapping**: See what the attacker is searching for and how they move

Done correctly, deception turns attackers into unwitting informants.

Psychological Impact

Deception is psychological warfare. It turns confidence into confusion and momentum into doubt. Deception is not just technical it's psychological warfare. Attackers begin to doubt everything:

- Was that credential real?

- Is this host a honeypot?

- Have I already been seen?

Paranoia slows decision-making. Fatigue leads to mistakes. Deception inserts fear and doubt into every move. And in prolonged operations, doubt is more destructive than any exploit.

Strategic Integration

For deception to work, it can't be obvious. It must be:

- **Integrated** into the fabric of your network

- **Silent** until interacted with

- **Subtle** enough to trigger interest but not suspicion

Deploying deception is not a gimmick—it's strategic defence through narrative control.

The best trap is the one they walk into thinking it's their idea. With deception, you don't just defend—you influence. You don't just detect, you shape. Deception isn't defence. It's design... With deception, you don't just defend, you influence. You don't just detect, you shape. And in the shadows of misdirection, you reclaim control of your network.

Next, we turn to attribution and the high-stakes game of naming your adversary or letting them believe they've named the wrong one.

Chapter 10: Attribution and the Great Game – Naming the Ghost

Attribution is the theatre of cyber warfare. It's where intelligence meets narrative, and shadows are assigned masks. In espionage, naming the ghost matters but choosing *which* ghost to name can be a weapon in itself... It's where intelligence meets narrative, and where shadows are given names. In the world of cyber espionage, knowing *who* is behind an attack can be more valuable than knowing *how* they did it. But the truth? Attribution is as much theatre as it is tradecraft.

This chapter explores the complexities, the risks, and the manipulation inherent in the attribution game. Because in the murky world of global cyber conflict, the wrong name can start a war, and the right one can win one.

The Layers of Attribution

True attribution is never based on a single indicator. It's layered, corroborated, and deeply contextual. It includes:

- **Technical Evidence**: Malware artefacts, IP addresses, C2 infrastructure, binary signatures

- **Behavioural Indicators**: Tactics, techniques, and procedures (TTPs) consistent with known groups

- **Temporal Patterns**: Working hours, language settings, compile times

- **Infrastructure Reuse**: Domains, certificates, or server configurations previously tied to other ops

- **Human Intelligence (HUMINT)**: Sources that confirm the identity or origin behind a campaign

The best attribution combines multiple sources across technical and geopolitical intelligence.

False Flags and Plausible Deniability

Good operators know they're being watched. Sophisticated adversaries will:

- Embed false language settings

- Use misdirection in compile times or time zones

- Reuse other groups' tooling

- Route through compromised infrastructure to throw off scent

These techniques muddy the waters inviting strategic miscalculations, misattribution, or diplomatic fallout. They are the digital equivalent of throwing a stone and pointing at someone else. In the geopolitical arena, they don't just mislead analysts they can manipulate national responses, distort intelligence consensus, and shift public perception. Good operators know they're being watched. Sophisticated adversaries will:

- Embed false language settings

- Use misdirection in compile times or time zones

- Reuse other groups' tooling

- Route through compromised infrastructure to throw off scent

These techniques muddy the waters inviting strategic miscalculations, misattribution, or diplomatic fallout. They are the digital equivalent of throwing a stone and pointing at someone else.

The Attribution Pipeline

Each phase of attribution introduces risk not just of technical error, but of narrative bias. What starts as analysis can become influence. Attribution is rarely done by one person. It's a process:

1. **Collection**: Pull logs, malware samples, telemetry, and intelligence reports

2. **Correlation**: Align findings with known indicators, actors, and infrastructure

3. **Analysis**: Weigh probability, identify gaps, rule out bias

4. **Narrative Construction**: Frame the findings in context for stakeholders, media, or policy makers

Often, the attribution report becomes a strategic tool not just an intelligence product.

The Political Edge

Attribution doesn't just provoke action it shapes posture. It influences diplomatic relations, cybersecurity policy, and future deterrence strategies. Attribution changes how governments and corporations respond:

- APT linked to a nation-state may trigger sanctions or diplomatic action

- Criminal groups might face law enforcement pursuit

- Public attribution can deter future operations or provoke retaliation

Sometimes, the goal isn't even accuracy. It's influence. Perception becomes more powerful than proof.

Counter-Attribution as Tradecraft

Just as defenders try to name, attackers try to avoid being named. Counter-attribution techniques include:

- Rotating toolkits between campaigns
- Using public exploits rather than custom ones
- Laundering infrastructure through multiple jurisdictions
- Avoiding persistent infrastructure reuse

The best actors leave no signature. Or better yet they leave *someone else's*.

In espionage, knowing who you're fighting matters. But in cyber warfare, it's not always about truth. It's about the story. Attribution isn't just naming the ghost it's deciding which ghost to name, and which illusion to let live. In this game, truth is optional. Plausibility is power.

Next, we explore the human side of operations: manipulation, profiling, and the art of digital recruitment.

Chapter 11: The Human Factor – Profiling, Manipulation, and Digital Recruitment

Behind every terminal, every password, every compromised account there's a person. And people are the most vulnerable component in any security system. Cyber espionage may begin in code, but it ends where it hurts most in human psychology. Because the most valuable vulnerabilities aren't technical. They're emotional, behavioural, and personal. This chapter dives into the human terrain: how targets are profiled, manipulated, and sometimes even recruited.

Because espionage doesn't just exploit systems it exploits people.

Profiling the Target

Just as systems are scanned for weaknesses, people are reconned for pressure points. Profiling continues the reconnaissance process but turns it inward, toward the human element. Before you can manipulate a target, you must understand them. Profiling builds a complete psychological, professional, and behavioural portrait. Techniques include:

- **Social Media Analysis**: Interests, routines, political affiliations, emotional triggers
- **Professional Footprints**: Job titles, reporting lines, certifications, conference talks
- **Personal Metadata**: Geolocation from photos, relationship status, family connections
- **Credential Leaks**: Password habits, reused credentials, historical logins

Profiling isn't just intelligence it's pretext fuel.

Building the Pretext

Once a target is profiled, attackers craft believable scenarios, pretexts to guide the victim's behaviour. These might involve:

- Fake recruiters offering dream jobs
- Vendor impersonations requesting logins
- Colleagues asking for help via compromised channels
- HR or IT support running "urgent updates"

A successful pretext blends seamlessly with the target's reality.

Exploiting Cognitive Bias

Psychological insight is the catalyst that turns access into control. Biases make humans predictable, and predictability is exploitable. People aren't logical machines. They're creatures of habit, emotion, and bias. Understanding psychological levers makes manipulation easier:

- **Authority Bias**: Messages from a perceived superior are obeyed

- **Scarcity Bias**: Limited-time offers or expiring access trigger urgency

- **Trust Transference**: If it comes from a known domain, it must be safe

- **Familiarity Bias**: Brands, names, or platforms the user already trusts

The most potent payloads ride in on trusted assumptions.

The Digital Recruitment Model

This isn't just about gaining access it's about creating psychological dependency. Recruitment blends trust, manipulation, and incentives into long-term control. Sometimes, cyber espionage doesn't just want data it wants people. Digital recruitment involves identifying and nurturing potential assets:

- Engage anonymously through forums or professional networks

- Offer tools, guidance, or exclusive intel to test loyalty

- Progressively request access, files, or credentials

- Build dependency, incentive, or leverage

By the time the asset realises they've been recruited, it's often too late.

Defending Against the Human Exploit

The best technical defence can be undone by one click. Defending against human-targeted espionage means:

- **Security Awareness Training**: Not just compliance modules, but real scenario-based engagement

- **Simulated Attacks**: Red team exercises, phishing simulations, insider threat drills

- **Access Controls**: Least privilege, role-based access, and separation of duties

- **Behavioural Monitoring**: Detecting sudden changes in user access or communications

Educated users aren't perfect but they're harder to turn.

The human mind is the original attack surface unpatched, unmonitored, and often unseen. It can be mapped, influenced, and exploited more easily than any machine. In espionage, the best exploit isn't code. It's trust and it's almost never detected... It can be mapped, influenced, and exploited sometimes more easily than any machine. In espionage, the best exploit isn't code. It's trust.

Next, we look at the operational lifecycle how long-term campaigns are structured, maintained, and closed with precision.

Chapter 12: Operational Lifecycle – Orchestration, Maintenance, and Closure

Espionage isn't a one-off event it's a cold war in miniature. A long-term campaign unfolds like a shadow script layered, persistent, and invisible until it's too late. From the first whisper of recon to the last digital fingerprint wiped, elite intrusions are orchestrated with patience and precision... A long-term operation unfolds over weeks, months, or even years. From the first bit of recon to the final deletion of artefacts, the most successful intrusions are meticulously planned, dynamically executed, and surgically retired.

This chapter explores how elite cyber operations are orchestrated, maintained, and ultimately closed without a trace. It's the long game measured not just in impact, but in silence.

Phase 1: Planning and Reconnaissance

This phase mirrors what we covered in early chapters reconnaissance, profiling, and strategic targeting but here it's wrapped into an operational timeline. Every campaign begins with information and intent. Every operation begins with a blueprint. Target selection, objective setting, and risk assessment are all front-loaded:

- Define mission scope: data theft, disruption, surveillance, or influence
- Profile target systems, personnel, and third-party links
- Select tooling and infrastructure appropriate for stealth, speed, or persistence

Time spent in planning saves time in execution—and reduces the chance of detection.

Phase 2: Access and Establishment

Once recon validates the pathway, the breach begins. This phase includes:

- Gaining initial access via phishing, exploits, or social engineering
- Deploying first-stage implants for foothold
- Establishing communication channels for command and control

At this point, persistence mechanisms are laid, and the first breadcrumbs are planted.

Phase 3: Expansion and Elevation

With presence secured, the operator spreads:

- Privilege escalation to gain broader access
- Lateral movement to discover valuable systems and pivot points

- Internal reconnaissance to map critical assets and relationships

Each move must be stealthy, calculated, and logged for operational memory. This internal record written for the operator, not the logs ensure continuity, enables learning, and protects the mission from internal drift.

Phase 4: Objective Execution

This is where mission goals are fulfilled:

- Data collection and staging

- Surveillance of internal communications

- Sabotage or influence operations

Timing is critical. Operations may span weeks of surveillance before extraction or disruption is triggered.

Phase 5: Maintenance and Surveillance

Long-term operations require care:

- Rotate infrastructure and refresh malware signatures

- Monitor for signs of discovery or investigation

- Update C2 protocols and adapt to environmental shifts

Good tradecraft means keeping one foot on the gas and the other on the brake.

Phase 6: Closure and Sanitisation

Closure isn't just about clean-up it's about denial. It's narrative control. The goal isn't just to leave it's to erase the fact you were ever there. Exfiltration may not end the campaign. Closure includes:

- Erasing logs, forensic artefacts, and local files

- Withdrawing implants and C2 infrastructure

- Closing down user accounts or false identities

- Restoring normal system states

Clean exits are as important as quiet entries.

An operation isn't judged solely by what it achieves but by how little it reveals. The best operations leave nothing but questions in their wake. Like ghosts, they slip through systems and disappear before the story is even written.

In the final chapter, we step back. What does it all mean? What comes next? The future of espionage is already here. It's time to look forward.

Chapter 13: The Future of Espionage – AI, Autonomy, and the New Shadow War

Espionage has always evolved with technology from whispers and parchments to satellites and malware. But this next leap isn't evolution it's mutation. It's not just new tools. It's intelligence that operates without us. from smoke signals to encrypted satellites, from dead drops to digital implants. But the next leap is different. It's not just about new tools. It's about intelligence that learns, adapts, and operates independently.

The future of cyber espionage belongs to autonomy and artificial intelligence. Human intuition will still matter but machines will scale operations, hide deeper, and strike faster than any human team ever could.

AI-Driven Recon and Targeting

Automation transforms the hunt. With AI, reconnaissance becomes constant, adaptive, and nearly invisible. Entire networks can be assessed in moments campaigns that once took weeks will take seconds. Tomorrow's operators won't manually gather OSINT or trawl through breach data. AI agents will:

- Crawl, correlate, and contextualise public and private data at speed

- Profile targets with behavioural precision

- Flag vulnerable systems and high-value assets across broad networks

This isn't science fiction it's already happening. The difference will be scale, autonomy, and stealth.

Offensive Autonomy

Future offensive frameworks will think for themselves:

- Select optimal access vectors based on environmental scanning

- Deploy adaptive payloads depending on real-time defence posture

- Adjust C2 protocols and timing based on observed detection heuristics

These aren't just scripts they're strategic agents. Pre-programmed initiative, with real-time feedback loops.

Deepfake Deception & Cognitive Ops

Perception becomes the battleground. Truth is optional. Narrative is everything. As trust erodes online, deception evolves:

- Deepfake audio/video to impersonate leadership or insiders

- AI-written phishing with hyper-personalisation

- Synthetic social personas to build influence and infiltrate organisations

Psychological operations will scale like spam once did only far more believable.

Defensive AI and Counter-Autonomy

The defenders aren't standing still. AI will:

- Detect novel attack patterns beyond human correlation

- Isolate and contain threats in real time

- Monitor user behaviour and device baselines with extreme sensitivity

- Predict lateral movement before it begins

Defensive AI becomes the new firewall but faster, smarter, and evolving.

Shadow Wars and Attribution Fog

As explored in Chapter 10, attribution becomes even harder when ghosts write their own signatures. With autonomous systems on both sides, operations may: With autonomous systems on both sides, operations may:

- Launch without explicit human approval

- Trigger faster than policymakers can respond

- Be harder to attribute due to synthetic signatures

The shadow wars of the future won't just be hidden they'll be silent, fast, and deniable by design.

The future of espionage is no longer about *if* it will change. It's about *how fast*. Intelligence won't just be gathered it'll be grown, shaped, and deployed in milliseconds. The ghost doesn't knock anymore. It compiles, executes, and vanishes before the alarm ever sounds... It's about *how fast*. Intelligence won't just be gathered it'll be grown, shaped, and deployed in milliseconds. The ghost has learned to code. And now, it thinks.

This is the new frontier. Welcome to the next theatre.

Chapter 14: Case Files & Black Missions – Fictionalised Ops from the Field

The best way to understand cyber espionage isn't through theory it's through stories that mirror the chaos and craft of the real world. This chapter presents fictionalised missions inspired by real-world tradecraft. Each scenario walks through the operation step by step, annotated with tactical commentary and red team insight.

These are not stories for entertainment. They are training missions in disguise.

Mission: Emberlight

This mission highlights a high-value theft operation executed with precise timing and minimal noise.

Objective: Steal design blueprints from a defence contractor's internal R&D network without tripping detection.

Background: The target is a Tier-1 aerospace firm with heavy segmentation, advanced monitoring, and behavioural analytics. However, several of their remote engineers use personal devices for off-hours development.

Phase 1 – Recon Passive OSINT reveals usernames, conference speakers, and GitHub commits. One engineer posts screenshots with blurred windows, metadata reveals the hostname and internal IP range.

Tradecraft Commentary:

- Metadata extraction is one of the most overlooked OSINT sources.

- Engineers are high-value targets due to their mix of access and informality.

Phase 2 – Initial Access A poisoned PDF mimicking a CAD file is sent via a spoofed vendor domain. The engineer opens it late on a Sunday night. Macro triggers silent beaconing to a dormant C2 node.

Tradecraft Commentary:

- Timing matters. Off-hours access reduces alert fatigue.

- Vendor impersonation worked due to earlier profiling.

Phase 3 – Expansion The implant uses PowerShell to enumerate local credentials. Password reuse enables lateral movement to a staging server with access to the SVN repositories.

Phase 4 – Execution Files are zipped, encrypted, and fragmented. DNS tunnelling exfiltrates the data in 50kb chunks over two days.

Phase 5 – Closure Logs are timestomped. C2 infrastructure is dismantled. A dummy login failure loop is introduced to mask the previous connection trails.

Outcome: No alert was triggered. The blueprint was gone before Monday's login.

Mission: Halcyon Cross

This is a masterclass in restraint long-term infiltration without triggering a single defence mechanism.

Objective: Plant a covert backdoor in a foreign government ministry's IT procurement system.

Overview: The goal is long-term access, not immediate gain. Mission must be low-noise and persistent.

Phase 1 – Insertion An open-source developer with ties to the target is compromised. His public code contributions are weaponised malicious update routines added to a popular driver module.

Phase 2 – Supply Chain Deployment A contractor unknowingly pulls the tainted module during procurement system updates. Internal scan doesn't flag it.

Phase 3 – Establishing Persistence The payload only activates under specific OS builds and geolocation signatures. Once inside, it establishes HTTPS-based C2 disguised as telemetry data.

Phase 4 – Surveillance Mode No data is touched. Screenshots, keystrokes, and internal traffic are logged and exfiltrated slowly over a three-month period.

Phase 5 – Quiet Fade When the host OS is updated, the implant deactivates itself and wipes all traces.

Outcome: The operator has three months of insider intelligence without writing a single file to disk.

Each mission in this chapter demonstrates different tradecraft principles timing, targeting, deception, restraint, and escape. These are simulations, but they're grounded in real tactics. Use them to sharpen your threat modelling, inform red team exercises, or test your own operational flow. timing, targeting, deception, restraint, and escape. These are simulations. But they're built on truth.

Train your mind to walk through the op.

Next, we arm you with tools: how to build your own espionage capability from the ground up.

Chapter 15: Building a Cyber Espionage Toolkit – Trade Tools of the Silent War

You've seen the tradecraft in motion. Now it's time to understand the engine behind it. The tools don't make the operator, but they shape how far, how fast, and how silently one can move... Now it's time to look behind the curtain. This chapter breaks down the key tools, frameworks, and resources that underpin modern cyber espionage operations offensive and defensive. Whether you're constructing your own red team capability or training for clandestine ops, this is your technical foundation.

This isn't a shopping list. It's a blueprint.

Core Offensive Frameworks

These frameworks form the backbone of most multi-phase campaigns from initial compromise to internal dominance. Used together, they enable modular, adaptive, and persistent intrusions. Every serious operator needs a solid exploitation and post-exploitation toolkit:

- **Cobalt Strike**: The industry standard for adversary emulation. Beaconing, lateral movement, post-ex capabilities.

- **Metasploit Framework**: A modular, flexible exploitation engine with payload builders, scanners, and shell management.

- **Sliver**: A modern C2 framework with HTTPS, DNS, and mTLS communication.

- **Mythic**: A multi-implant C2 platform used for advanced tradecraft and scripting.

- **Empire (and Starkiller GUI)**: PowerShell-focused C2 framework. Useful for fileless persistence and LOtL operations.

Pair these with sandboxed VMs, proxy chaining, and encrypted tunnels.

Reconnaissance and OSINT Tools

These are your first line of intelligence. Combined with profiling tactics explored in Chapter 11, they allow you to map both systems and people before you engage. Surveillance begins with passive intelligence:

- **SpiderFoot / Maltego**: Automated mapping of people, domains, IPs, and leaks.

- **Recon-ng**: Modular OSINT framework for harvesting emails, creds, and hosts.

- **theHarvester**: Simple, reliable name, domain, and email collection.

- **Shodan / Censys / FOFA**: Internet-wide device scanning and exposure mapping.

- **Google Dorking + Custom Wordlists**: Still one of the most powerful recon tactics.

Master these before you write a single line of malware.

Covert Comms and C2 Infrastructure

Staying connected without being seen:

- **Cloudflare tunnels, Ngrok, or SSH over Tor**: Quick setup for covert callback channels.

- **DNSCat2 / Iodine**: DNS tunnelling for deep exfiltration.

- **Gophish or Evilginx**: Credential harvesting via phishing campaigns.

- **Domain fronting / CDN abuse**: Hiding C2 inside legitimate platforms.

Your comms setup should evolve per target profile.

Payload Development & Evasion

Evasion is not a phase it's an arms race. Staying ahead of defensive tools means continuously refining how you deliver and cloak your code. Bypass is survival:

- **Veil / Shellter / Unicorn**: Payload obfuscation and AV evasion tools.

- **Donut / NimPackt**: Shellcode generation and transformation.

- **Obfuscation Frameworks**: Invoke-Obfuscation, Invoke-CradleCrafter for PowerShell payloads.

- **BYOVD (Bring Your Own Vulnerable Driver)**: Kernel-level bypass with signed drivers.

Avoid signatures. Craft behaviourally.

Scripting and Automation

Glue code and automation are where operators earn their edge:

- **Python + PowerShell**: Still king for custom tooling and quick tasking.

- **Bash / Golang / Nim**: Lightweight execution and cross-platform support.

- **AutoHotkey / AppleScript**: GUI automation and local exploits.

- **Task Scheduler / Crontab / Systemd**: Persistence via native scheduling.

Script to replicate, to react, to adapt.

Building Your Own

Once you've learned the tools, build your own:

- Start by modifying open-source implants

- Learn how to write custom loaders and wrappers

- Design flexible, disposable infrastructure

- Maintain versioned TTP playbooks for reuse

Building capability isn't about having the best tools it's about understanding the ones you wield. Precision beats abundance. Discipline beats noise. The ghost isn't built from gear it's built from intent.

Next, we close the loop on tradecraft. The final chapter looks at life in the shadows: how to disappear, how to survive, and what it takes to walk away clean.

Chapter 16: Becoming a Ghost – Tradecraft for Modern Operators

In the world of cyber espionage, getting in is easy staying invisible is the art. In a digital terrain lit by telemetry and laced with traps, true mastery lies in never leaving a trace... Staying hidden operationally, technically, and psychologically is the real skill. This chapter explores what it takes to *become a ghost* in a digital world that's always watching.

The mission may end, but the need for invisibility doesn't.

Operational Security (OPSEC)

OPSEC is the thread that binds every stage of an operation from planning to exit. If you fail here, nothing else matters. Your first and last line of defence is you.

- **Compartmentalisation**: Isolate tools, personas, and infrastructure.
- **Burn Discipline**: Rotate infrastructure, discard compromised tools and build disposables.
- **Metadata Hygiene**: Strip EXIF, document trails, and digital fingerprints.
- **Noise Management**: Avoid patterns in C2, timing, and tool usage.

The best way to stay hidden is to behave like you were never there.

Disappearing Digitally

Technical vanishing is only half the work. The rest is in your habits discipline in action, sustained over time. Vanishing from the grid is harder than ever but not impossible.

- **VPN Chains, Mixnets, and Proxies**: Layered anonymity for daily operations.
- **Ephemeral OS Environments**: Live OS tools (Tails, Whonix) with zero persistence.
- **Disposable Infrastructure**: Cloud assets, domains, and endpoints spun up and torn down with precision.
- **Attribution Confusion**: Borrow techniques, languages, and tooling from other threat groups to muddy the trail.

Being anonymous is a technical skill. Staying that way is behavioural.

Post-Operation Hygiene

Once a mission is over, the true clean-up begins:

- **Data Exfil Logs and Local Artefacts**: Purge every access point and file trail.

- **Command Histories and Timestamps**: Timestomp or scrub shell logs and execution records.

- **C2 Closure**: Retire infrastructure methodically, with misdirection if needed.

- **Credential Rotation**: Never reuse; change all operational identities post-op.

Leave nothing behind but uncertainty.

Psychological Resilience

You can teach tradecraft, but mental resilience must be forged. Ghosts don't crack under pressure they disappear into routine. Living in the shadows takes its toll:

- **Routine Discipline**: Daily habits reinforce clean execution.

- **Emotional Distance**: Separate mission from identity.

- **Controlled Paranoia**: Always question, but don't collapse under doubt.

- **Exit Strategy**: Know when to walk, before you're forced to run.

Tradecraft isn't just skill it's mindset.

You don't become a ghost by disappearing. You do it by never being seen. Not by force, but by design.

This isn't the end. It's the beginning of a new state of being.

Welcome to the grey space. Stay there. Live there. Operate like you were born in the static... You do it by never being seen.

This isn't the end. It's the beginning of a new state of being.

Welcome to the grey space.

Appendices – Echo Black: Field-Ready Extras

These appendices are designed to extend the book into a practical field reference. They're living tools—meant to evolve alongside your tradecraft. Keep them close. Update them often. And when in doubt return to tradecraft... Keep them close. Update them often. And when in doubt return to tradecraft.

Glossary of Terms

Use this as a fast-access reference during operations, training briefs, or tool development sessions. A concise reference to common phrases, tools, and techniques in cyber espionage:

- **OPSEC**: Operational Security – procedures and habits used to maintain secrecy.

- **C2**: Command and Control – systems used to communicate with compromised assets.

- **LOtL**: Living off the Land – using native tools for stealth.

- **TTPs**: Tactics, Techniques, and Procedures – behavioural patterns used in attribution.

- **Beaconing**: Regular communication from a compromised host to a C2 server.

- **Burn**: To retire, destroy, or discard a compromised asset or identity.

- **Payload**: Code delivered to a target for execution (e.g., malware, implants).

- **Pivoting**: Moving laterally within a network post-compromise.

- **EXFIL**: Exfiltration – the act of extracting data from a compromised environment.

Standard Operating Procedures (SOPs) & Red Team Checklists

Designed for use in mission prep, threat simulations, or post-op debriefs. Adapt these to your operational environment. Field-tested and adaptable for your own missions.

SOP: Initial Recon and Target Profiling

- Identify key personnel, roles, and surface assets

- Gather passive OSINT and infrastructure details

- Correlate breach data or credential leaks

- Map probable access points and high-value assets

SOP: Compromise and Establish Foothold

- Select tailored initial access method (phishing, exploit, etc.)

- Deploy lightweight beacon and validate C2 comms

- Confirm user permissions and local system profile

- Lay minimal persistence with misattributed code

Checklist: Stealth and Persistence Hygiene

- Strip metadata from all created documents

- Avoid reusing C2 infrastructure between missions

- Vary timings and tools per host

- Timestomp logs and maintain noise discipline

- Burn any exposed tools or identities immediately

Checklist: Operation Closure

- Wipe C2 nodes and orphaned agents

- Scrub all artefacts from local systems

- Rotate or delete all operational credentials

- Close any used infrastructure providers

- Reassess for attribution artefacts

Further Reading & Resources

Explore with a critical mind. Think about how each source could translate into operational reality. Curated sources for deeper understanding and continued development.

Books

- *The Cuckoo's Egg* – Clifford Stoll

- *Countdown to Zero Day* – Kim Zetter

- *This is How They Tell Me the World Ends* – Nicole Perlroth

- *Sandworm* – Andy Greenberg

Websites & Projects

- MITRE ATT&CK (https://attack.mitre.org)

- HAK5 & SecurityTube

- Reddit: r/netsec, r/OSINT, r/ReverseEngineering

- Awesome-Redteam GitHub repo

Podcasts & Talks

- Darknet Diaries

- Malicious Life

- DEF CON / Black Hat YouTube archives

Your toolkit is your shadow. Keep it light, sharp, and ready to vanish... Learn them. Adapt them. Then disappear.

Thank you for reading this book.

Notes

Notes

Notes

Notes

Notes

Notes